With Illustrations for Comprehensive Learning

THE STORY OF ADMIRAL YI SUN-SIN

MADE EASY — For Kids and Adults Alike!

Woosung Kang

AF110777

Copyright © 2025 by Woosung Kang

All rights reserved. No part of this publication may be reproduced, distributed, or transmitted in any form or by any means, including photocopying, recording, or other electronic or mechanical methods, without the prior written permission of the publisher, except in the case of brief quotations embodied in critical reviews and certain other noncommercial uses permitted by copyright law.

For permission requests, contact us at:

marketing@newampersand.com

ISBN 979-11-93438-22-0

& **NEW AMPERSAND PUBLISHING**
newampersand.com

For more amazing titles

"Waaah! Waaah!"

A long time ago, in 1545,
a baby boy was born in Geoncheondong (now part of Seoul)
during the Joseon dynasty, and he let out a loud, hearty cry!

His name was Yi Sun-sin!

Yi Sun-sin was an energetic child who loved playing with his friends.

Sometimes, he even played mischievous pranks on adults and enjoyed horseback riding.

But Yi Sun-sin had a special dream.

"I will become a general who protects my country!"

From a young age, he had strong determination.

So, Yi Sun-sin began training to master martial arts.

He practiced archery with strength,
swung his sword with precision,
and trained on horseback.

After even more hard work, four years later, in 1576, at the age of 32, Yi Sun-sin challenged the military exam again and proudly passed!

At first, Yi Sun-sin was given a small position managing soldiers. But he never neglected training and always cared for his soldiers to help them grow stronger.

Above all, he was always honest and followed principles.

One day, a high-ranking official named Seo Ik gave Yi Sun-sin an unfair order and asked him to do something illegal for his own benefit.

But Yi Sun-sin firmly replied,

"We must uphold the nation's laws and principles."

Because of this, Seo Ik held a grudge against Yi Sun-sin and wanted to take revenge, so he submitted a false report!

"Yi Sun-sin is not managing the military properly!"

Hearing this, the royal court dismissed Yi Sun-sin from his position. Imagine how unfair this must have felt for Yi Sun-sin!

But he did not give up.

"One day, I will protect Joseon again."

Fortunately, four months later, Yi Sun-sin was reinstated as a general!

But he had to return to a lower rank than before.

"It's okay as long as I can serve the country!"

Yi Sun-sin never gave up his determination to protect his country. And a few years later, he was tasked with defending Nokdundo, a small island at the mouth of the Duman River, beyond which lay the land of the Jurchens.

"I must defend this place at all costs!"

General Yi Sun-sin fought bravely for his country and people. However, a military commander in North Hamgyeong Province named Yi Il falsely accused him!

"Yi Sun-sin failed to protect Nokdundo!"

In truth, General Yi Sun-sin had requested reinforcements beforehand, but the royal court did not grant them.

The king and his officials knew that Yi Sun-sin had fought bravely despite being outnumbered. But they couldn't avoid punishing him because of political reasons.

In the end, Yi Sun-sin was flogged and stripped of his military rank, serving as a common soldier in the war.

But because Yi Sun-sin gladly accepted the punishment, even though it was unfair, it showed his loyalty to the king and the nation, making a strong impression on King Seonjo and the royal court.

"This general is no ordinary man! He will fight for our country until the end!"

In 1591, Yi Sun-sin was appointed as the Naval Commander of the Left Jeolla Province!

Now, he had the important role of leading the Joseon navy from the Left Jeolla Naval Base (present-day Yeosu).

"It's time to head back to the sea!"

On April 13, 1592, the Japanese army gathered off the coast of Busan and launched their attack!

Joseon was thrown into chaos by the sudden invasion.

The Japanese army quickly captured Busan and Dongnae, then marched toward Hanyang (present-day Seoul).

The Joseon army fought back but kept losing, and eventually, King Seonjo had to flee far north to Uiju.

But admiral Yi Sun-sin had already sensed that war was coming and had prepared in advance.

In May 1592, Commander Won Gyun, who was defending the waters off Goseong in Gyeongsang Province, urgently requested help from Admiral Yi Sun-sin.

Without hesitation, Admiral Yi Sun-sin set out with about 80 ships.

When they reached the waters off Okpo, around 30 Japanese ships with red and white flags were floating there.

Some Japanese soldiers were looting villages on land and setting them on fire.

After their great victory at the Battle of Okpo, Admiral Yi Sun-sin's fleet sailed past Geoje Island and headed toward the waters off Yeongdeungpo.

Just then! An urgent report came in:

"GENERAL! FIVE JAPANESE SHIPS ARE PASSING BY!"

Admiral Yi Sun-sin immediately turned his ships around and began chasing the Japanese fleet.

Sailing swiftly in pursuit, they finally arrived at Happo (present-day Jinhae).

However, when the Japanese soldiers saw the Joseon navy approaching, they abandoned their ships and fled to land!

At dawn the next day,
the Joseon navy received more critical information:

"THERE ARE JAPANESE SHIPS AT GORIYANG IN JINHAE!"

Admiral Yi Sun-sin and Commander Won Gyun split their fleet into two groups and set sail.

When they arrived at the waters off Jeokjinpo, they found 13 Japanese ships anchored and resting! Admiral Yi Sun-sin shouted,

"Now is our chance! Attack!"

The Joseon navy bravely charged in and destroyed all 13 ships without leaving a single one behind.

On May 29, 1592,
Admiral Yi Sun-sin and the Joseon navy once again faced the Japanese fleet off the coast of Sacheon in South Gyeongsang Province.

The Japanese navy had brought 13 ships in total — 12 large warships and 1 smaller vessel — to seize control of the sea.

But this time, the Joseon navy had a very special weapon!

It was none other than the legendary Turtle Ship!

The Turtle Ship was covered in iron armor from bow to stern, making it impervious to enemy arrows and bullets.

Admiral Yi Sun-sin had studied, improved, and transformed this ship into an even more powerful weapon!

Leading the charge with the Turtle Ship, the Joseon navy fiercely attacked and destroyed all 13 Japanese vessels!

However, during the battle,
Admiral Yi was shot in the left shoulder by a bullet.

Even so, the admiral ignored his pain and fought until the very end, leading his fleet to another glorious victory!

On June 2, 1592, another fierce battle broke out off the coast of Dangpo in Tongyeong, South Gyeongsang Province.

Led by Admiral Yi Sun-sin,
the Joseon navy triumphed once more,
defeating 21 Japanese warships!

Three days later, the Joseon navy pursued the Japanese forces to Danghangpo, also in Goseong, South Gyeongsang Province.

The Japanese navy, defeated at the Battle of Dangpo, had fled to Danghangpo to hide.

However, when the Japanese soldiers saw the Joseon navy approaching, they abandoned their ships and fled to land!

Admiral Yi Sun-sin first sent three ships to carefully scout the area. And the report came back:

"The Enemy is here!"

Admiral Yi Sun-sin immediately gave the order to attack!

The Joseon navy fearlessly charged in, destroying all 26 Japanese ships and defeating countless enemy soldiers, including their commander.

Thanks to Admiral Yi Sun-sin and the Joseon navy, the sea remained safe, and many Japanese forces were driven back.

Five days later, the Joseon navy spotted the Japanese fleet off the coast of Guyulpo, Geoje Island!

Admiral Yi Sun-sin led 23 ships,
Admiral Yi Eok-gi led 25 ships,
and Admiral Won Gyun led 3 ships,

making a total of 51 Joseon warships chasing the Japanese fleet!

The Japanese navy was heading to Busan with five large ships and two medium-sized vessels.

But as the Joseon navy rapidly pursued them, the Japanese tried to escape to land!

However, they could not outrun the speed of the Joseon navy!

In the end, all seven Japanese ships were destroyed, and their commander, along with many soldiers, fell in battle.

"Hooray…! Hooray…!"

The sea still belonged to the Joseon navy!

In July 1592, the Japanese army tried to advance to Gadeok Island, located between Busan and Geoje Island.

The Japanese Supreme Commander, Toyotomi Hideyoshi, gave the command to his soldiers:

"CRUSH THE JOSEON NAVY!"

In response,
the Japanese navy gathered about 70 ships and assembled in the narrow strait of Geonnaeryang, between Geoje and Tongyeong!

But… Geonnaeryang was an incredibly narrow and dangerous place!

Admiral Yi Sun-sin, however,
took advantage of this and prepared a brilliant trap!

Admiral Yi Sun-sin sent some warships into Geonnaeryang to lure the Japanese navy. As the Joseon army intentionally retreated, the Japanese thought:

"HAHA! THE JOSEON ARMY IS FLEEING!"

and chased after them toward Hansan Island!

At that moment!
Admiral Yi Sun-sin struck the drum and commanded,

"LIKE A CRANE SPREADING ITS WINGS!"

The Joseon navy spread out in a circular formation, using the "hak ik jin" tactic!

The turtle ships led the charge, and other battle ships followed! And the Joseon navy completely surrounded the Japanese forces!

As a result, 59 Japanese ships were destroyed! Japan lost 9,000 soldiers, and the remaining soldiers hurried to flee!

Yet, the Joseon navy lost not a single ship!
This victory forced the Japanese to abandon their plan to circle around the southern coast and head toward the western seas!

A great victory achieved through the wisdom and courage of Admiral Yi Sun-sin!

Admiral Yi Sun-sin headed to the sea once again!
Off the coast of Angolpo, near Changwon and Jinhae in South Gyeongsang Province, the Joseon navy defeated 81 Japanese ships!

The Japanese forces found it increasingly difficult to transport and supply their troops, and the Joseon navy was steadily advancing toward Busan!

On September 1, 1592, this time the Joseon navy headed toward Busanpo, the Japanese forces' stronghold.

"There are so many Japanese troops on land, and there are a huge number of ships at the shore!"

The Japanese had anchored no less than 470 ships at Busan! Admiral Yi Sun-sin pondered,

"How can I fight against such a large force?"

"Yes, a surprise attack is what we need!"

The Joseon navy, led by Vice Admiral Jeong Un, charged first!

"Fire! Sink the ships!"

At the fierce assault from the Joseon navy, the Japanese forces were caught off guard and rushed out to sea.

But since they were unprepared, over 100 of their ships were swiftly destroyed!

However, during this battle, the brave Vice Admiral Jeong Un was killed... But Admiral Yi Sun-sin could not afford to dwell on his grief.

"Let's avenge Jeong Un!"

Soon after, Admiral Yi Sun-sin led another attack and continued his victories, defeating the Japanese navy at the Battle of Uengpo and the Second Battle of Danghangpo!

Through these victories, the Joseon navy completely cut off the Japanese supply lines!

Led by Admiral Yi Sun-sin, Yi Eok-gi, and Won Gyun, the Joseon navy fought the Japanese forces from February 10 to March 6, 1593.

By defeating over 100 Japanese ships, the Joseon navy once again achieved a great victory!

Now, the Japanese forces in the southern seas began to feel the pressure and crisis mounting.

One year later, the Japanese forces were moving toward Danghangpo in Goseong, South Gyeongsang Province.

A fleet of 31 ships was heading toward Danghangpo. But Admiral Yi Sun-sin couldn't stay idle!

"Unfold the "hak ik jin" formation!"

The Joseon navy surrounded the enemy using the "hak ik jin" tactic, like a crane spreading its wings.

"Fire the fire arrows!"

With flaming arrows and cannons, the turtle ships charged! All 31 Japanese ships were sunk, and the Joseon navy achieved a perfect victory!

The Japanese forces in the southern seas were gradually disappearing, and the Joseon navy relocated their headquarters back to Hansan Island.

After victories at the Battle of Uengpo and the Second Battle of Danghangpo, the seas around Joseon were once again safe!

Admiral Yi Sun-sin was now appointed as the Commander of the Three Provinces' Naval Forces, overseeing the navies of Gyeongsang, Jeolla, and Chungcheong Provinces!

In 1594, Japan was negotiating peace with Joseon and the Ming Dynasty. However, the Japanese forces remained stationed in the southern seas, showing no intention of ending the war.

As a result, the Joseon army decided to launch an attack to completely drive out the Japanese forces.

At Jangmunpo, the navy led by Yi Sun-sin and the army led by Gwak Jae-u and Kim Deok-ryeong joined forces. But the Japanese forces hid in the fortress on Geoje Island and refused to move.

The Joseon fleet tried to lure the Japanese forces out, but the Japanese did not want to fight. The Japanese forces focused solely on defending their fortress on land, avoiding battle at sea.

In the end, the Joseon forces only managed to destroy two small Japanese ships without a major battle.

But a problem arose!

This battle wasn't led by Admiral Yi Sun-sin but by Yun Du-su, the Commander of the Three Provinces, and other brave generals also opposed the battle, considering it to be an overly risky move.

However, Won Gyun accused Yi Sun-sin of deliberately failing to fight and blamed him for not engaging actively!

As a result, a situation began to form that was unfavorable for Yi Sun-sin. Despite still being ready to fight for the country and its people, political traps were slowly pushing him into a crisis.

Joseon, Ming, and Japan were still engaged in peace talks to end the war.

However, Japan's demands were so unreasonable that in September 1596, the negotiations broke down.

As a result, in 1597, Japan invaded Joseon once again.

This was the "Jeongyu War," the second war of the Imjin War!

Just before the war resumed, a great crisis befell Admiral Yi Sun-sin.

Hearing rumors that the Japanese forces were heading toward the southern seas, the Joseon court ordered Yi Sun-sin to capture the enemy commander.

But Yi Sun-sin responded with caution, saying,

"This might be a trick by the Japanese..."

Once again, Won Gyun accused Yi Sun-sin of disobeying royal orders, claiming he did not follow the king's command.

As a result, in March 1597, Yi Sun-sin was unjustly arrested and imprisoned.

He underwent harsh interrogation for 28 days and was facing the threat of execution.

However, the civil vassal Jeong Tak pleaded,

"Yi Sun-sin is a hero of the nation. He must be spared."

Thanks to his plea, Yi Sun-sin avoided execution, but he was stripped of his official position and dragged to the battlefield as a soldier.

From that point on, he became a soldier without a rank.

Despite this, the Joseon court ousted Yi Sun-sin and appointed Won Gyun as the Commander of the Three Provinces' Naval Forces.

The question remained:

Can Won Gyun defend Joseon properly…?

After Yi Sun-sin was framed and imprisoned,
Won Gyun became the Supreme Commander of the Joseon Navy.

However, unlike Yi Sun-sin, who was a cautious strategist,
Won Gyun was reckless and greedy as a leader.

In the end, in July 1597, the Japanese navy launched another large-scale attack, and Won Gyun faced them without proper tactics.

As a result, the Joseon navy was almost completely destroyed, and important commanders like Lee Eok-gi and Choi Ho were lost. Not surprisingly, Won Gyun also died.

Moreover, out of the 130 ships in the fleet, 120 were sunk, and nearly all of the 13,000 Joseon soldiers were wiped out, with only around 10 ships managing to escape.

That's right. The Joseon navy, which Yi Sun-sin had built up, was destroyed in an instant!

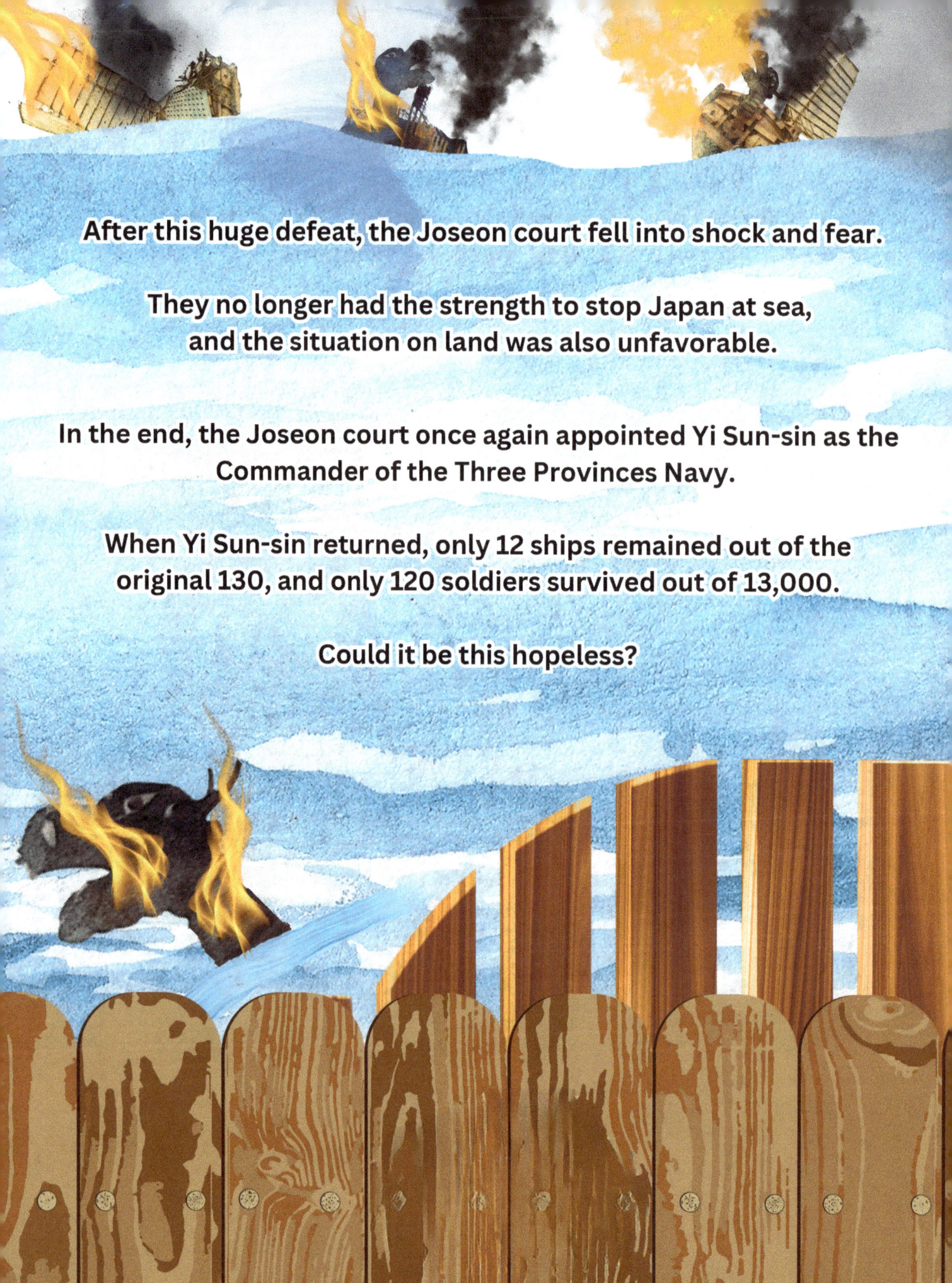

After this huge defeat, the Joseon court fell into shock and fear.

They no longer had the strength to stop Japan at sea, and the situation on land was also unfavorable.

In the end, the Joseon court once again appointed Yi Sun-sin as the Commander of the Three Provinces Navy.

When Yi Sun-sin returned, only 12 ships remained out of the original 130, and only 120 soldiers survived out of 13,000.

Could it be this hopeless?

The Japanese army believed the Joseon navy was completely gone.

At that time, the court decided to disband the navy and only keep the army to fight.

But Admiral Yi Sun-sin did not give up.
He submitted a report to the king, saying,

Impressed by Admiral Yi Sun-sin's strong will,
the court decided to maintain the Joseon navy.

Moved by his determination, the soldiers began to gather one by one, and they started collecting weapons little by little.

Kim Eok-chu, the military officer of Jeolla Province,
joined with a single ship, bringing the total number of ships to 13.

However,
this was an absurdly small number compared to Japan's 133 ships.

"How can we overcome this disadvantage?"

Admiral Yi Sun-sin decided to fight at Uldolmok (Myeongnyang Strait).

This place had narrow and rough waters, shaped like the neck of a bottle, where large ships could not easily move.

The waters of Uldolmok flowed quickly, making a loud sound.

Here, large ships could not maneuver easily. Yi Sun-sin thought:

"If we fight here, we can win!"

By morning, Japan's massive fleet of 133 ships pushed into the Myeongnyang Strait.

"HA HA! NOW THE JOSEON NAVY IS FINISHED!"

The Japanese forces were confident,
thinking their numbers would guarantee victory.

At that moment,
the ship carrying Admiral Yi Sun-sin boldly moved to the front!

Yi Sun-sin shouted,

"Those who seek death shall live, those who seek life shall die!"

Emboldened, the Joseon navy fired large cannons and flaming arrows, launching an assault on the Japanese fleet.

"Take these fire arrows!"

The arrows rained down like a storm upon the Japanese ships.

"HUH? THE SHIP ISN'T MOVING AS IT SHOULD!"

Due to the swift current, the Japanese ships collided with each other and swayed.

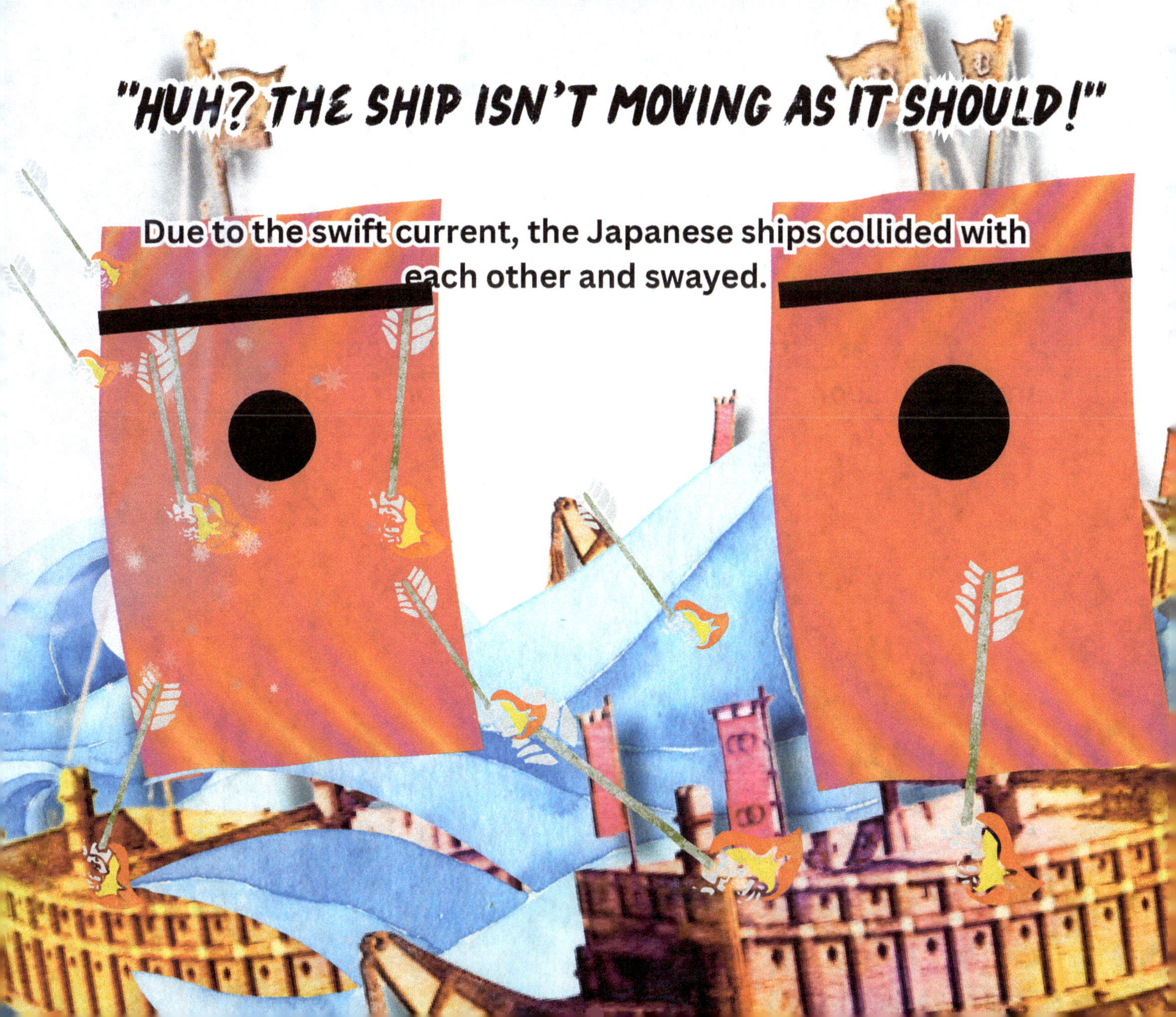

At that moment, the ships led by Kim Eung-ham, reinforcing the Joseon forces, joined the battle!

"Admiral! We will help you!"

With renewed strength, the Joseon forces fought even harder against the Japanese.

A miraculous victory! When the battle ended, all 13 Joseon ships had survived! However, 31 Japanese ships sank, and many others were damaged beyond repair or fled in retreat.

It was a victory so miraculous that it seemed almost unbelievable!

As a result, the tides of war turned, and the Joseon navy began to reclaim control of the seas.

After suffering a great defeat at Myeongnyang in 1597,
the Japanese forces retreated to the southern coast of Korea.

In the following year, 1598, when Toyotomi Hideyoshi of Japan
passed away, the Japanese decided to withdraw from Joseon.

To return safely, the Japanese secretly bribed the Ming general,
Jin Lin, asking him to turn a blind eye and allow their safe passage.

At first, Jin Lin considered granting their request.
However, Admiral Yi Sun-sin strongly opposed, saying,

**"We cannot allow the Japanese forces
that tormented Joseon to leave
without consequences!"**

Impressed by General Yi Sun-sin's bravery, Jin Lin decided to join forces with him to block the Japanese retreat.

"This is the path the Japanese must take. We must stop them here!"

Admiral Yi Sun-sin hid the Joseon and Ming navies on both sides of the strait, waiting for the enemy to approach.

In the dark of dawn, the Japanese forces launched a surprise attack!
However, Admiral Yi Sun-sin was already fully prepared.

"Now! Attack!"

Arrows rained down like a storm,
and the massive warships were engulfed in flames.

"AHH! RETREAT!"

The Japanese forces panicked and tried to fall back,
but the path had already been blocked.

"We defend the seas of Joseon!"

General Yi Sun-sin and his soldiers fought fiercely, engaging the advancing Japanese forces in a final, intense battle.

At that moment!

A bullet from the Japanese forces struck Admiral Yi Sun-sin, and he collapsed!

Despite the pain, Admiral Yi Sun-sin, concerned for his country and his fellow soldiers, urged them on.

"Do not speak of my death while the battle is still raging..."

His voice, filled with concern for his nation, echoed over the sea.

The general's nephew, Yi Wan, shouted,

"Let us fight until the end for the admiral!"

and led the soldiers into battle.

Ming general Jin Lin, moved to tears, whispered,

"Oh... Admiral Yi Sun-sin..."

The Joseon navy and Ming forces were filled with grief at the death of Admiral Yi Sun-sin, and the entire sea seemed to echo with the sound of mourning.

Wherever the funeral procession of Yi Sun-sin passed, the people wept and grabbed hold of the carts, unable to let them move forward.

He was 54 years old at the time.

With this final battle, the Japanese forces completely withdrew from Joseon.

And the war with Japan,
which had lasted for seven years,
finally came to an end.

After Admiral Yi Sun-sin passed away,
the king bestowed upon him the posthumous title "Chungmu."

This title combined the meaning of "Chung," representing loyalty,
as it signifies protecting the ruler even in the face of danger.

Meanwhile, "Mu" refers to military prowess,
symbolizing the defeat of invading enemies.

It serves to forever honor and commemorate Admiral Yi Sun-sin!

He was a hero who fought without fear of losing his life,
dedicating everything to protect the people and the country
against Japan's invasion.

충무
이순신

Today, in Seoul, South Korea, there is a street named "Chungmu-ro," named after Admiral Yi Sun-sin's posthumous title.

In the heart of Seoul, at Gwanghwamun Square, stands a massive statue of Admiral Yi Sun-sin, holding a sword in one hand and standing tall with a fierce expression, symbolizing his bravery.

Both Koreans and foreigners who gaze upon this statue are reminded of the sacrifice, loyalty, and boundless love Admiral Yi Sun-sin had for his country and people.

It's a legacy that continues to be etched in their hearts.

Korean History Made Easy - For Kids and Adults Alike!
With Illustrations for Comprehensive Learning

Available on Amazon

www.ingramcontent.com/pod-product-compliance
Lightning Source LLC
LaVergne TN
LVHW062050070526
838201LV00080B/2290